LINDSEY MCNEAR

Healing Generations : The Painful Pivot

Contents

Preface

I've constructed a new identity for myself. Peeling back the masks I've had to wear to survive in a world where I had to keep everyone around me comfortable.

If I were to change too much they wouldn't feel okay about themselves and that's scary to a lot of people. it's hard to sit with yourself and feel through your own demons.

I'm an independent spirit that wants to understand the world, so come along with me as I take you into my example of what you can do for yourself to peel back what you can find in your own soul's purpose as you live out your lifetime here on Earth.

Acknowledgments

A special thanks to my spirit team and ancestors for leading me intuitively to accomplish my earthly goal of writing a book that helps reshape humanity.
May my legacy continue in generations to come.

1

What Your Upbringing Never Taught You

Healing to a human body is natural and it knows how to respond once you give it the correct environment to mend and thrive. To me, the human body is quite interesting. I believe there is a lot we still don't know about how it truly operates. Our vessel carries the emotional memories, regrets, fears, joys, excitement, anxiousness and anger. It holds on to all of the good, bad, and ugly we have ever known. Think of it like the hard drive to a computer.

The biggest key to healing is to sit in stillness so you can hear what your intuition is guiding your soul to do. Some think that this is a special power that only some carry. The truth is, it is within us all.

We can heal from within when we slow down, realize what we have held inside of us for years or even generations and make the first step to change how we see it. Pain travels through families until someone is able to feel it.

A person doesn't really get desperate about waking up to a different life perspective until something traumatic happens to them directly, to which they absolutely cannot live like that anymore.

This could be a near death experience, a bad health issue, or a close loved one passing. It's almost like a switch goes off in you and you just refuse to continue on believing this is the only way life can be.

When this happens, it is called a spiritual awakening. It changes your life forever. You start seeking inside of yourself. Asking, "How can I love myself better?".

It happens differently for everyone and continues to happen over and over again through the years, showing each person a little bit more about life.

Healing has many different modalities as I will explain a few in this book to help guide you but you have to pick what works best for yourself.

Most of all, see what your body and mind responds to the best. You may find other ways that work better for you and that's awesome too!

It's all about listening to your intuitive guide from with in. Everyone holds something different and that is what makes you uniquely beautiful.

2

Self Realization : How Did I Get Here ?

J an 29, 2022. My dad left this earth with none of his family around to set him free. He laid alone, intubated in the ICU on the 6th floor of our local hospital. Suffering from multiple health issues that caused him to be admitted, but then he contracted coronavirus which lead to his isolation and ultimately, his death.

After caring for my father for six years and seeing his health decline each season, I was instantly relieved that his body could rest. I was happy he didn't have to fight for another breath or struggle to do a small task. I felt bad for being happy that his worn out flesh could be laid to rest.

Even though I could only talk deeply about it to my partner, I knew I shouldn't feel bad about my relief of him passing.

When you see someone go through several surgeries for cancer, weeks of chemo treatments, daily breathing treatments, inhalers, a pill box you've never dreamt of and countless nights in the hospital, you want it to end for them.

Having such bad health, It turns into torture. I would constantly wonder "Is he okay?". "Is he still breathing?".

Waking up in the middle of the night to check on him.

My parents divorced when I was sixteen years old. I chose to stay living with my dad in our childhood home. My three other siblings chose to live with my mom a few blocks away. As I witnessed my dad go through the darkest time of his life because of my mom's choice to leave him, he shared with me his biggest fear.

He feared having no one there to help him when he got older. Someone that would care enough to look after him when his body was aging and he couldn't fully make clear decisions.

I didn't really know what that felt like because I was so young and had not thought that far into my future but I vowed in my heart to always take good care of my dad when he got older and that is just what I did.

See, I'm a natural nurturer. I naturally can take great care of people. I make people feel comfortable, accepted and loved. This seemed like an easy task. He's my dad. Little did I know it would last six years and take a lot of self sacrifice. I sacrificed more than I needed to but it was a full time job making sure he had what he needed.

I was consumed with going to the pharmacy, grocery store, doctors appointments and everything in between while I was also raising a young boy. My days off turned into my second job. The days I worked turned into a space of reprieve. My roles in life were opposite of the standard house hold.

I am a seasoned hairstylist, being in the industry for 21 years,

I have built a clientele that makes it easy to work around life circumstances. This is what allowed me to take care of my dad so well.

No one talks about how much life is taken from you as a care taker. I put my own health on hold to make sure he had what he needed. Since I had my youth I didn't think too much of it until he passed and I looked at myself, what my body needed, and what my child missed out on. It threw me!

To mother a child, try to have friendships, run a business and care for a loved one. Dating was kind of out of the question. For I didn't have the time to give, much less it be exciting and fun.

Once I was released from any and all responsibilities dealing with my parents care and passing I would overthink everything about my life and so much anger would build up. I was so relieved but super unhappy inside.

Close friends and family would tell me it's a stage of grief and it would soon leave and I wouldn't have to endure it any longer. Just to give it time. They had clearly never been in this situation themselves to know how deeply bothering it is.

I wasn't having it. I knew the stages of grief as I had to endure them many times in my life both personally and professionally.

I feel like it was my body screaming for me to pay attention to it. It needed nurturing because of so many years of lack. At first I had no idea what kinda of wild ride I was about to go on!

3

Self Action : How Do I Pull Myself Out of This?

I would sit in my living room and write vigorously in my journal about all the things gone wrong, my frustrations, and how I needed to vent.

I am second in line of four children. My mother passed away at the young age of sixty with stage four lung cancer just two years before my father. It was fairly traumatic for all of us as it spread to her liver, spleen and bones. After the diagnosis we only had two short months to spend with her. Most of which were spent at our local hospital and the hospice hospital where she passed away.

I would be irate that I could not seem to pin point the emotional trail I had created. I couldn't get to the stem of what really was pissing me off. I mean, yes, I knew there were things I needed to work through but I had not a clue on where to begin. I felt so alone in what I was dealing with because no one had a road map I could follow or a step by step program that would fulfill my needs personally.

As a child born in the eighties, I was never taught how to effectively process my emotions on a healthy level, which caused me to stuff those emotions. I figured it was just a German quality I had inherited. I just accepted my immediate family was all just like that.

Until I learned that over time it causes us physical pain and a lot of discomfort from with in. The body keeps a record of all of those feelings we never expelled through allowing ourselves to actually feel them, kept safety in our fascia. A thin lining wrapped around each muscle and organ in our bodies.

When I zeroed in, I went from victim mentality to asking myself what I could really do to help myself heal. I knew most of this problem I was having was going to have to be solved by myself. I always could blame the best of them for anything, so this took a lot of self reflection. I knew that I didn't want to sit in front of a counselor for the next two years twiddling away at my feelings. Telling someone my history and my current feelings is fine and healthy but I knew I wasn't going to get far with that approach this time.

I needed cold hard healing and scientific help on how to exude this energy from my everyday body.

The internal struggles we all have and keep hold of, no one else has a clue about are hard to bring to the surface at times. I needed this more than I ever thought.

Recognizing I was angry, filled and fueled by anger. I was so absolutely pissed that my whole world was nothing I had ever experienced before. Flipped inside out of what I knew for thirty-eight years. All I knew, in these moments was I needed to change it.

I could feel the stress of the world zinging from with in me. Every breath I took was short and shallow. My mind would race about other people's thoughts of me. Interactions I would have, would live within my mind for days. I would think so badly of how I reacted to people or hear their words replay in my mind. I would think about how I should have responded differently. It was hasty though.

Nothing I thought of was loving.

After multiple days of waking up exhausted, I was scrolling on social media and I came across a doctor talking about the benefits of Magnesium Lysinate Glycinate. He recommended taking three to four hundred milligrams at bedtime with a tall glass of water right before you shut your eyes, so this would be the very last step in your bedtime routine. So I figured I would try it.

When I tell you this changed my whole life, I mean it. I used to never be a morning person and all of a sudden I was okay with getting up early. My body felt alive again. I was well rested when I woke up so there was no need to lounge in bed anymore. I could get up, exercise and do my daily tasks.

After about a week of taking magnesium and resonating with videos online I thought this might just be helpful as I heal. Which leads us to the moment everything shifted for me in my life as I knew it.

The next video that resonated with me was one from a younger guy telling me about how one night right before bed asked spirit for his vibration to be heightened. I thought well that seems kind of weird. I knew from science that everything is energy and how everything holds a different vibration but I never really thought about the human experience being molded around that exact vibration. Let alone that you could ask God to heighten it for you.

So on that night, I did the same thing. I asked God to make my vibration higher. At the time, I had no idea what I was getting myself into but I wouldn't go back to that life if you asked me to.

I didn't notice a lot at first but I believed something would change. I continued to resonate with videos online and it was like my spirit guides were showing me piece by piece how to put my puzzle back together again. This healing I was experiencing at a higher consciousness was a much different path than when my mom passed away. It was a much more peaceful and vibrant experience. Although I missed my parents, my soul was released from seeking any sort of parental approval. I could be my authentic self.

I would soon discover that this is called a spiritual awakening.

After seeing a video online, I taught myself how to reset my central nervous system so that my body could begin healing itself from the traumas life had handed me. Your CNS is your first line of defense in the body. If this is on high alert, the body cannot calm, relax or use any sort of natural healing because it's being triggered. It is its job to protect, not mend.

I learned that the nerves in your eyes are attached to your vagus nerve which goes from the base of your neck to the end of your tailbone. Scientifically, it helps the body protect itself. Spiritually it keeps track of any and all traumas from the day you are born. It's a very interesting nerve.

Mine was very disregulated. I loved distraction, always was stressed about nothing. Always had an anxious thought and feeling about something going on around me.

So, with a simple sixty to ninety second exercise I could reset my CNS at any time during my day to calm my breathing, and relax my body to a point it could bring healing.

At first, I would do this a couple of times per day. Then as my body would become used to being in its parasympathetic state I wouldn't have to use it as often.

Who knew that the nerves in the eyes could be so powerful? I've included the steps below if you'd like to try this at home.

Resetting Your Central Nervous System:

I sit calmly in my chair. Turning my head all the way to the right and then all the way to the left.

Do you feel discomfort? Most people do. They have a tight neck or shoulders.

Bend your elbows and place your hands on the back of your neck.

Looking straight ahead, crank your eyes all the way to the right and keep that stare until you yawn, gasp or sigh. Then do the other side to the left until you have the same reaction. This usually takes about a minute on each eye to release.

You will instantly feel the calmness come over your body. I like to then take a deep breath in and out appreciating what my body had just done for me.

The CNS is your body's first line of defense when it feels unsafe. So, allowing it to calm down and know it is safe, you can then attempt healing.

I taught myself how to properly breathe again. Crazy right? A lot of us, if not all of us, are walking around shallow breathing. It's the bodies response to the trauma we feel. Anxiousness, stress, panic, our body is saying something is wrong. So we take shorter breaths in our diaphragm.

It all correlates with the central nervous system being off course. As a society we are in fight or flight all the time.
I would put up sticky notes around my home to remind me to deep breathe as I would go about my day. Taking in enough air to fill your lungs and hold it for a few seconds. Then a long exhale. This will retrain your diaphragm to relax. Until one day I realized I had been doing it naturally and then could take them down. It really is amazing how quickly the body will learn and unlearn different practices we give to it.

Just as most things we do as a habit can be changed. So can your body, & mind. Following your intuitive nudges is the key to living the path your soul came here to truly accomplish. We didn't sign up to come to earth, just to survive evil.

Soon after, I scheduled a Reiki session with a local practitioner. Reiki is a Japanese form of energy healing. Guided by an instructor to release held or stored energy in the body not serving us well.

She talked with me about the burdens I carried. She explained how the body has an extra layer outside of our shell that carries what is called our energy body. Others may recognize it as being called the Human Energy Field (HEF)

She explained how it extends about 6 inches past where we see our outline of the body in the physical form.

The practitioner taught me about using meditation to clear our main seven chakras and how it relates to having good energy health. Clearing those chakras daily would keep that energy body in good health.

I was excited at this point to have something new and useful to focus on in my healing journey.

As the practitioner guided her way through our session I could feel where the emotion was being released where I had been holding on to it the most. In my right pelvic area and leg. In my case it caused my leg to quiver as it left my body. I was fascinated.

I felt so thankful for her knowledge and the time she took to explain each step for me. As I added this practice to my mornings I felt more calm and nourished with in.

Next, I would meditate for at least 5-10 minutes per day. Allowing my body to move as intuitively as she needed to. Discharging emotions I didn't know I had. One day I might be crying with sadness or laughing with joy. Each day was different. I would somatic dance, self manipulate massage, use EFT tapping, sound healing and other modalities depending on what I was feeling. The biggest part is to allow your body the time and feeling of what it needs to do that day.

I grew up in a traditional household. We attended a non-denominational Christian church. In my spiritual upbringing I was never taught about energy, energy being stored in the body and how if effected us physically. This made a shift in my perspective on how to handle what I was feeling and more of what my body was needing me to do for it mentally. The signals were finally understood. This made sense now.

Learning trauma can be stored in the fascia of our muscles of the body. This was a big realization to me.

Feeling appalled and betrayed that my chiropractor and physical therapists through out 18 years had never told me this but they are taught that in school.

I had spent so much money and time to maintain a body that could have been helped permanently through knowing this.

I learned about grounding in nature and how to dispel all of my extra energy that was revving me up continuously. Getting back to nature was so important.

My ancestors and spirit guides really needed me to see the importance of this step.

I thought it was stress or caffeine but it was really extra energy wanting to be let out. Walking in nature to see the treasures and signs from passed loved ones like my parents or to walk barefooted to ground my energy or place a hand on a tree trunk in my back yard was actually so calming. Basically, touching anything that connects your bare skin to Mother Earth safety with out harmful temperatures to expel the extra is what our bodies need. You can touch the snow or my ultimate favorite is to take a healing swim in the ocean. Think of the earth as our human charging station but ultimately it does the opposite. We just simply need to make the connection important again.

Another small but useful insight, especially while being around the general public for your job, is clearing your energy for the day and protecting it from bringing in bad or nervous energies. Call it witchy if you will but being a hairstylist this has helped me a ridiculous amount!
   Learning how to clear my energy from the day before, take back the power I hold and protecting my energy from others around me that could potentially siphon it subconsciously.

When people take your energy, you'll feel tired, drained and unmotivated. These practices have helped me be the most for the people around me to complete my day effectively while giving the most to each individual.

I like to use this mantra when I clear my daily energy. You can use this as much or as little as you would like during your day but the long term key is to believe it was done the first time. Believing in yourself and in your higher self.

"Wipe away, Wipe away all bad energy of today. You have to go, you have to leave. Calling all power, all power back to me now. Putting up my biggest and highest protection for today. And so it is"

This takes care of clearing, believing you have the power and always knowing you're protected in your soul's walk for the day.

4

Human Distractions

When the psyche has an overwhelming list of tasks or just things to remember for you during your days, it has no room to question any behaviors let alone heal family trauma.

I had to quiet my mind, reset my nervous system, and create movement in my body so that my mental clarity could guide me in ways to start the healing process.

It's super easy to take on more people pleasing tasks so you can look good in a community, than to sit and face the hard questions your soul needs answered.

As you heal, you will realize the behaviors of the people closest to you fairly quick. The American way has been taught to us by taking a pill, putting on a cream or running more tests to see what is wrong. The American way is to drink on the weekends, take a hit off of our weed pen and try to forget the life we are actually living. Just to make it another day is the goal most of the time. No one seems to be really enjoying their earthly experience.

The medical professionals were never taught that there is so much more to do with the body and our emotions that they cannot always tell us why we are in pain. You have to figure it out on your own through time, being alone and getting to re-know your body in a way that is so spiritually sacred. A place that no one can tell you any different.

You own all of the rights to how you feel in your own skin. You just need to be present.

My own personal experience with this was fighting pelvic pain. For six years I viewed it as a medical problem in my body. It was very painful on the front right side. Sometimes veering to the top of my pelvic bone and then sliding into my low back.

I really blamed this on standing for a living, not wearing the correct shoes, or maybe I could blame it on lifting heavy things at times.

None of which was really true. I still to this day am working through getting that area completely healed but what I realized was it was family trauma on my dads side that is being held so tightly that it's a hard one to let loose.

Once I figured out it was a lot deeper than just the body needing regulated I sure had an easier time with it.

For me personally, it has been decades of anger held with in the family. I was taught that the liver actually holds the anger and if your liver energy meridians are not open, it cannot flow down and out to be released. I'm the one to feel it and heal it. In my case I am the families black sheep. I am my family's healer.

Generations worth of madness being released through my quiet oneness. Think of all the generations in your lineage that could never speak their truth. Think of the generations to never feel free in their own skin. To never be able to know what it feels like to sit in peace so they could reflect. Imagine that for a moment.
In my case, I'm so thankful I can provide my body with the environment to expel all that has been held. I was the one to feel the pain. I wear my accomplishments proudly. It has been an honor.

On the body, your right side is the masculine/ father's side and the left side is the feminine/ mother's side. If you always remember that part it's a little easier to work through the pains and what you're trying to evaluate. In regards to the brain, it is opposite. Left side father, right side mother.

Just because you have the knowledge of how to heal doesn't always mean the course of your healing will be short nor easy but having the right tools sure helps!

5

Finding Support As You Feel Alone

As I learned to love myself better I felt all of my close friends slide by. I soon realized that I would be the one to call or text to initiate dinner plans or just to chat. As I made more distance between them by not communicating to them first it led to a gap in the relationship. I would hear people discuss how these "friends" would hang out with different friends of theirs and find time for fun things going on in our city. All the while it was sure quiet on my end.

I learned about quantum entanglement and how some just are not cut out to be close to us once we realize their motives. Whether they were just hanging out to get something out of me, get a discount on hair services or just lingering. I couldn't just sit there and let all the things happen. I quickly cut the cord to any and all people close to me that didn't make me feel good anymore. When you're in control, you get to choose. The people that you get in front of that just make your stomach ache or make you worry about doing the wrong thing in front of. Those are the ones you'll want to let go of.

It was my central nervous system telling me something was wrong! I no longer had the patience or tolerance for any more bullshit to happen to me in my life. Spirit would show me who was doing me wrong and who was okay. It feels like a super power once you get a little practice in.

I was thankful for the true friends that sought me through this time. That would lend an ear and not call me crazy for thinking differently than them.

My partner would also be a supportive, listening ear while knowing full well some of the things I would talk about he didn't fully see the same as me but was always there.

I found comfort in listening to podcasts. Seems silly but it kept me from being depressive as I was so different than most people around me after making this big change of perspective. I truly felt alone except when I would hear their stories and what they had going on in life. I needed to hear from like minded people and that's where I would connect.

I was lucky enough to have a couple of clients and a good friend that were on the same page as me as I walked thru my transition of healing and learning to ride the wave with me but not everyone will have that.

I would reprogram my mind with using words of affirmation daily. Telling myself the good I wanted to believe again. I would use the same phrases for days at a time. Changing when I felt ready to shift to the next. Just as you would remember bible verses as a child you can reprogram your mind like a computer to reclaim the self worth and knowing of your souls purpose.

I am a big believer that you will always have what you need as you journey your path through life. God will provide the proper people and strategies to help get you to the next point you need to be at. Just like this book.

I may have people say to others "She just isn't the same person anymore" and for that I am proud. That means I have done the work internally and it is being shown to the world physically. As each one of us heals internally, it changes the vibration of the earth. It reflects in a way that you can't comprehend. It is said to heal seven generations before you and seven generations after you. As a whole we get closer to having a calmer way of life. Peace on earth.

I have recovered from people pleasing and I am so glad to have regained respect for myself as I set new boundaries. As life turns another page, I hope you find a little bit more ease in navigating your healing journey, as I created this book with you in mind.

Be authentically you, that's what makes you beautiful.

Afterword

If Healing Generations resonated with you, a review helps this book find others who are ready to heal. I love to hear from my readers!

Please note that I am not a licensed medical professional giving any medical advice. Nor do I claim that any medical diagnosis will be healed to one person specifically by using these modalities.

Thank you for being here.

About the Author

About the Author

Lindsey McNear is a writer, healer, and transformational guide devoted to breaking generational cycles and helping others reclaim their authenticity. Through lived experience, deep self-inquiry, and conscious healing, she explores how inherited patterns shape our lives—and how awareness becomes the doorway to freedom.

With a background rooted in human connection, creativity, and intuitive leadership, Lindsey blends personal storytelling with reflective insight, offering readers both honesty and hope. Her work centers on emotional healing, self-trust, and the courageous choice to evolve beyond what we were taught to carry.

Healing Generations is her deeply personal memoir and an invitation to heal not only for yourself, but for the generations that follow.